I MOVED
YOUR
CHEESE

I MOVED YOUR CHEESE

*For those who refuse to live as mice
in someone else's maze*

Deepak Malhotra

HARVARD BUSINESS SCHOOL

Berrett–Koehler Publishers, Inc.
San Francisco
a BK Business book

Berrett-Koehler Publishers, Inc.
235 Montgomery Street, Suite 650
San Francisco, CA 94104-2916
Tel: (415) 288-0260 Fax: (415) 362-2512 www.bkconnection.com

ORDERING INFORMATION
Quantity sales. Special discounts are available on quantity purchases by corporations,
associations, and others. For details, contact the "Special Sales Department" at the
Berrett-Koehler address above.

Individual sales. Berrett-Koehler publications are available through most bookstores.
They can also be ordered directly from Berrett-Koehler:
Tel: (800) 929-2929; Fax: (802) 864-7626; www.bkconnection.com

Orders for college textbook/course adoption use. Please contact Berrett-Koehler:
Tel: (800) 929-2929; Fax: (802) 864-7626.

Orders by U.S. trade bookstores and wholesalers. Please contact Ingram Publisher Services,
Tel: (800) 509-4887; Fax: (800) 838-1149;
E-mail: customer.service@ingrampublisherservices.com;
or visit www.ingrampublisherservices.com/Ordering for details about electronic ordering.

Berrett-Koehler and the BK logo are registered trademarks
of Berrett-Koehler Publishers, Inc.

Printed in the United States of America

Berrett-Koehler books are printed on long-lasting acid-free paper. When it is available,
we choose paper that has been manufactured by environmentally responsible processes.
These may include using trees grown in sustainable forests, incorporating recycled paper,
minimizing chlorine in bleaching, or recycling the energy produced at the paper mill.

Library of Congress Cataloging-in-Publication Data

Malhotra, Deepak, 1975–
  I moved your cheese : for those who refuse to live as mice in someone else's maze /
Deepak Malhotra. — 1st ed.
    p. cm.
  ISBN 978-1-60994-065-2 (hbk. : alk. paper)
  ISBN 978-1-60994-976-1 (pbk. : alk. paper)
  1. Organizational change. 2. Change (Psychology) 3. Compliance. 4. Didactic literature.
I. Title.
  HD58.8.M2452 2011
  650.1—dc23

                                                              2011022340

FIRST EDITION

17 16 15 14 13   10 9 8 7 6 5 4 3 2 1

Designed and produced by Seventeenth Street Studios
Copy editing by Karen Seriguchi
Cover designed by Leslie Waltzer/Crowfoot Design

To Aisha, Aria, and Jai . . .
here is what I most want you to know.

CONTENTS

DISCUSSION QUESTIONS

PREFACE

When a book has sold over twenty million copies, due respect for the opinion of its readers creates an obligation to explain why someone would seek to challenge its central message. I hope to do that, briefly, in these opening pages. The real answer, however, lies in the fable itself.

This book was written—and is meant to be read—as a stand-alone entity. Not surprisingly, however, I've been asked whether it was crafted as a rebuttal to *Who Moved My Cheese?* (*WMMC*), or as an extension of it. Or, to put it another way: Am I saying that the message of *WMMC* is incorrect, or simply incomplete? The answer is both.

For those who are having a hard time dealing with big (or even small) changes in life,

ix

WMMC is a compelling read. The book is a useful reminder that we need to accept that change happens, that it may be beyond our control, and that we need to find the strength to move on and adapt. This message is neither incorrect nor trivial. But it *is* incomplete. Even when adaptation appears to be the only viable option, we should do more than blindly accept— and eagerly adapt to—change. We should seek to understand why the change has been forced on us, how we might exert greater control over our lives in the future, whether the goals we are chasing are the correct ones, and what it would take to escape the kinds of mazes in which we are always subject to the designs of others. In other words, effective adaptation is not enough for success or happiness.

Then there are the ways in which the message of *WMMC* is not simply incomplete, but dangerous. Perhaps we should think twice before telling others that they would be wise to immediately embrace their limitations. Perhaps we should not suggest to would-be innovators, problem solvers, entrepreneurs, and leaders that instead of wasting their time wondering why things are the way they are, they should simply accept their world as given. Perhaps we should stop telling people that they are simply mice, chasing cheese, in someone else's maze. I know those are not the messages *WMMC* set out to promote, but to many readers, they are powerfully conveyed.

I Moved Your Cheese aims to help readers question their assumptions about what limitations they really face and to encourage them to take the steps necessary to change not only their behavior but also their circumstances. In the face of long-standing precedent, strong social norms, resource scarcity, and the powerful expectations of others, individuals may underestimate their ability to control their own destiny, to reshape their environment, and to overcome the constraints they face. Success in areas such as career development, innovation, entrepreneurship, creativity, problem solving, and business growth—and also personal growth—often depends on exactly that: the ability to challenge assumptions, reshape the environment, and play by a different set of rules . . . your own.

Like *WMMC*, this book tells the story of mice who live in a maze. In this case, the main characters are three unique and adventurous mice: Max, Zed, and Big. As we watch their lives unfold and intersect, we discover that instead of just reacting to change and chasing the cheese, each of us has the ability to escape the maze or even reconfigure the maze to our liking. We can create the new circumstances and realities we want, but first we must discard the often deeply ingrained notion that we are nothing more than mice in someone else's maze. As Zed explains, "You see, Max, the problem is not that the mouse is in the maze, but that the maze is in the mouse."

This book is intended for people and organizations who feel trapped in their current circumstances; for people who are working hard and maybe even finding success in their life and work, but who struggle to find meaning or fulfillment in what they are doing; for those who are playing (perhaps very well) a game that is not of their choosing; for those whose view of success is not simply predicated on changing the old ways of doing things but on reimagining them; and for those who seek inspiration as they consider what they can and should do with the rest of their lives. (And if you're unsure whether you fit any such description, just read the book—it's short!)

Max, Zed, and Big have been with me for a long time now. And yet every time I revisit their adventures, I find myself inspired anew. I hope you will be inspired as well. And more than anything else, I hope that reading this book will put a smile on your face—and that you will be left wondering exactly why you are smiling.

I MOVED YOUR CHEESE

THE GOOD BOOK

They called it a revolution. The lesson—the insight—had spread throughout the maze. Scarcely a mouse remained who had not heard what was contained in the good book.

The insight was profound. More importantly, it did not rely too much on one's ability to reason. And any mouse will tell you that this attribute is the hallmark of all great truths. So it was accepted as perhaps the greatest, and certainly the most important, truth. And it was all so simple.

The book made it clear: Change happens. You can sit there and complain about it, or you can change with the times. Do not fear change. Accept change. What happens in the maze is beyond your control. What you *can* control is your reaction.

Now, just because every mouse had come to understand this insight does not mean that every one of them was able to adopt it in practice. Some succeeded fully. They learned that change is inevitable and uncontrollable. They accepted that they were helpless to control the workings of the maze—fate, they called it— and they pledged to adapt.

Many others succeeded to a lesser degree. They still had moments of fear, immobility, depression, and despair. But such moments were less frequent than in the past. These mice improved their lot in the maze considerably.

To be sure, there were also mice who rarely thought about what the good book taught them. They agreed with it in principle but did not have the time or energy to change their ways. After all, habits are hard to break. They would work on it later—maybe next week, maybe next year.

Overall, life in the maze was now quite different. In the past, when cheese moved from one location to another, all the mice were in despair. They could not understand what happened. They cursed their luck. They sat and waited in the cheese corner of the past and prayed for its return. They got agitated and lost their temper. They got angry and made an already difficult life even worse.

Now, after reading the good book, the mice reacted differently. The disappearance of the cheese was still traumatic, and it was still impossible to understand why the cheese had moved. But now the mice began to go in search of new cheese depots. Those who had fully adopted the good book's philosophy were the first to set about in search of the new cheese.

Those who struggled with the philosophy, who found it difficult to break old habits, were slower to move. But they, too, understood that they had to change with changing times. They, too, eventually went to look for more cheese.

By learning to change with changing times, the mice succeeded in finding more cheese. They found it more quickly than they had ever done in the past. The good book was right! They had cheese . . . more cheese, and sooner than ever before. It does not get much better than that if you are a mouse.

And so the mice no longer questioned why

the cheese moved. Everyone agreed that such questions had no answers. They did not try to devise plans to try to stop the cheese from moving. Only a fool would think that fate could be controlled. Above all, they never again asked the unreasonable question, "Who moved my cheese?"

Life was simpler now. It all came down to a very simple equation:

You want cheese

+

The cheese is no longer here

= Go elsewhere to find the cheese.

After all, for a mouse in a maze, cheese is really all that matters.

But then . . .

Well ... then there was Max.

And Max was altogether different.

MAX

When Max was younger, he once asked his parents why there was a maze. His parents didn't understand the question. When he persisted, they told him that some questions have no answers and that the maze simply *is*. When he asked why the maze was designed the way it was, and why it had so many useless paths, they told him not to waste time wondering why. They told him to focus, instead, on learning how to navigate the maze. You don't get to the cheese by wondering why, they said; you get to it by running around the maze as fast as you can. The maze, they explained, was a *given*. You work with what you're given. It is pretty arrogant for a young mouse to think that he could do otherwise, they cautioned.

Max was not blessed with the virtue of blind obedience. Instead, he continued to annoy his parents, his friends, his teachers, and anyone else who made the mistake of discussing such matters with him. The more he questioned, the more he discovered how little the other mice understood. They *knew* a whole lot, but they *understood* very little.

One day Max came across the good book. It infuriated him. He could not figure out how such a book could be so widely read and so blindly accepted. Upon reading the book, all the other mice had resolved to accept change without question because change, it taught, was inevitable and uncontrollable.

But Max was different. And upon reading the book, Max resolved quite the opposite.

Max was determined to discover who had moved the cheese. He was determined to discover why they had moved it. He was determined to discover why the maze was the way it was. And he was determined to change what he did not like about the maze. And so he set about it.

And a long time passed.

ZED

Zed was a mouse who did not care much for cheese. He ate cheese because it helped sustain his body. And he cared to sustain his body mostly because it was needed to sustain his mind.

Zed had a reputation for being wise, although few mice had ever spoken with him in great depth. He was a popular mouse, but he usually only spoke on important matters when someone else initiated the conversation. Zed loved company, but he seemed to appreciate moments of solitude just as much.

Zed had a magnetic personality. He had a certain look in his eyes—and a half smile—that mesmerized his audiences. And an audience is what they were—the mice who visited him were there to be in his company, to hear him speak, to be rejuvenated. No one could quite explain why he had such an effect on them.

What they knew, and what every other mouse came to know, was that Zed was a mouse like no other. He did not care for cheese, he did not care to learn how to navigate the maze, and he did not feel compelled to follow the routines and customs of the other mice. Yet, somehow, it was clear that Zed loved his life—the life of a mouse—more than any other mouse they had ever known.

As a result, those who knew Zed—or had heard of him—simultaneously revered and feared him. They revered him because his mere presence—his manner of being—inspired them to be great. They feared him because he was living proof that someone who seemed to challenge their every belief about what was important could still be happy—and in fact, could be happier than any other mouse in the maze.

One day, on seeing Zed sitting quietly in one corner of the maze, a small group of mice gathered. As Zed lifted his eyes, he noticed that they were eager to speak with him. Zed had grown accustomed to such unplanned, informal discussions. He was accustomed to the way they began, the way they progressed, and the way they tended to end. He did not expect any surprises.

That, perhaps, is why they are called surprises.

WHY

One of the younger mice in the group spoke first.

"Zed," began the young mouse, "my friends and I were discussing the good book. We were talking about how we might learn to accept change—how we might get past idle speculation about 'why' change happens. You know, it is said that change is inevitable and cannot be controlled . . . Well, certainly you've read the good book. Anyway, my friend here mentioned that you do not care much for the book. That you do not really believe what it says. Which is—well, I must say that I think you're wrong. I mean . . . Of course, I want to hear why you would think so. Everyone says that you are a great thinker and that you are very wise. But . . . I know that you're wrong. How can you possibly reject the great insight of our age—of all ages! I was hoping—well, we were hoping to hear what you had to say about it. It's not true, is it? Do you disagree that change is inevitable?"

Zed smiled. "I do not disagree. The good book is quite right. Change is inevitable."

The young mouse was visibly relieved. He felt he should thank Zed. He was about to express his gratitude when Zed spoke again.

"I do not disagree," Zed repeated. "But I think it is unimportant. It is irrelevant."

The young mouse was stunned. He wished Zed had outright disagreed with him. Difficult as it is to hear that your thinking is flawed, it is much worse to hear that your thinking is pointless.

"How can you say that!" exclaimed the young mouse.

"Well," replied Zed, "let me start by asking you a question. You tell me that change is inevitable. What is so important about this insight of yours?"

"It . . . it tells us how to live. It explains what is important. It explains what we can control and what we cannot—so it helps us focus. It tells us how to make the best use of our time." The young mouse was beginning to gain confidence. "It teaches us to be efficient. It helps us become more effective. It does all of this—and perhaps more."

"Very well," said Zed. "That is an impressive list."

The young mouse looked pleased.

"Will you indulge me just once more?" asked Zed.

"Yes, of course," replied the young mouse.

"You say the insight explains what is important," started Zed. "Tell me—what have you learned is important? What have you been taught to focus on? What goal does the good book suggest you spend your time pursuing? What are you efficient at achieving? Your effectiveness is measured *by what standard?*"

The young mouse looked at him. He thought about answering each question in turn. He was preparing to do this—and then it dawned on him. There was one answer. The same one answer to every question Zed asked. And the young mouse fell silent, shocked by what he realized.

More mice had gathered by now. All eyes were on the young mouse. They were waiting for him to answer. They were getting anxious.

"Cheese," answered the young mouse. "The answer to all of your questions is cheese. That is what I have learned is important. It is what all of us have been taught to focus on. It is what we spend our time chasing. All we can control is how fast we run in search of cheese. The best among us are efficient at finding cheese. Our effectiveness—the standard by which we measure success—is just that: How much cheese do we have?" And then he added a final word. It was not in response to anything that Zed had asked. It was in response to the realization that overwhelmed him.

"Why," stated the young mouse solemnly. It was an answer—a conclusion—and not a question.

Zed smiled compassionately.

By now, the crowd was much agitated. They felt betrayed by the young mouse.

"What is the meaning of all this?" shouted an elderly mouse. "What is the point of this discussion? Who are you to decide what is relevant? Why, you agreed that change is inevitable—that it is uncontrollable—and—"

"I did not agree to that," interrupted Zed. "I did not agree that change is uncontrollable."

"If you disagree, then you're a fool," sputtered the elderly mouse.

"Perhaps."

The elderly mouse continued, angrily. "And what can be more important than this? What can be more relevant to a mouse than this?

Do you not wish for us to pursue what might make us happy?"

Zed continued to look at the young mouse. The young mouse had moved closer to Zed, away from the crowd. Zed looked at him, gently, and spoke, answering the elderly mouse but still addressing the young mouse.

"What I wish is not that you pursue happiness, but that you actually find happiness. Is it possible to pursue happiness if the pursuit itself does not make you happy?"

The young mouse answered, sadly: "No. Not in the maze. In the maze, there is only pursuit. It has no end. No matter how much cheese you accumulate, you keep running. You don't find happiness here. You only find more cheese."

The crowd was in despair. The elderly mouse took to the offensive.

"Those are fine words. But they are not worth much. A mouse must take the maze as given. All a mouse has to think about is how best to navigate this maze. And when the cheese moves, the only thing a mouse has to ponder is how to find it again. What would you have us ponder instead?"

Zed looked at the elderly mouse and smiled. Then he answered.

"Why, there are many more interesting and important things to ponder," Zed responded matter-of-factly. "Have you ever thought about *why* change is inevitable? Have you ever wondered *why* the maze is the way it is—what purpose it serves? Have you ever thought to ask *why* mice spend their entire lives in search of cheese? Have you ever wondered, upon finding it missing, *who moved my cheese?*"

The last of these struck the crowd. All at once the anxious mice began to retort—to shout:

"This is a waste of time."

"Why ask such questions?"

"It's preposterous."

"Ludicrous."

"Childish."

"Impractical."

"No one can know *who* moved the cheese."

"There is no answer to *that.*"

The crowd settled, and there was a brief silence.

And then, shattering the stillness of the moment, a voice from behind the crowd was heard. The voice was powerful, confident, and dispassionate—almost indifferent. But the words were spoken deliberately.

"I know who moved the cheese," it said. "And I know why they moved it."

EVEN THE "IMPOSSIBLE"

The crowd was aghast. They turned to see who had spoken those impossible words. They turned to see whether anyone would lay claim to such an utterance. They turned and saw Max. No one had seen him in almost a year. He was exultant.

Max was looking past the crowd—through them. His gaze was fixed on Zed. He did not seem to notice the crowd.

"I know who moved the cheese," Max repeated. "And I will tell you about it." He was speaking only to Zed.

The crowd was silent. They would have quickly disregarded the outburst as a lunatic's rant, but

Max had a look in his eyes that dismissed such a notion. Each of the mice, individually, knew that he was serious. As a group, they were unwilling to consider this possibility. They did not know what to think. They did not want to think. Each of them was waiting for someone else to do the thinking—for someone in the crowd to decide how they should all react. Finally, the elderly mouse snickered.

"How wonderfully absurd! We have no time for tall tales. We were having a serious discussion here. Awfully rude of you to interrupt us like that, don't you think? Well, we won't be baited by your silly remarks. Come, friends. This discussion is going nowhere. And it's getting late. I, for one, have better things to do."

The elderly mouse had spoken with marvelous eloquence, especially considering how unsure he was of his own words. And the other mice were grateful for his effort. Slowly, the crowd dispersed. They had lingering doubts about whether they should leave, but those doubts would vanish in time. In a week, the entire episode could be forgotten. Except, perhaps, by the young mouse.

Only Zed remained after the crowd had dispersed. He had not moved at all. Max approached him.

"I would like to speak with you," said Max.

"I am quite sure that I will want to hear what you have to say," replied Zed.

"It has been quite a year," continued Max. "So much has happened. I have seen so much. I have learned and done so much. Zed, you are the first mouse I have encountered who I am sure will understand what I have to say—and what it signifies. Will you listen?"

"Yes."

Max walked toward Zed and sat next to him. He noticed that Zed looked very young. He had heard of Zed and had expected to find someone much older.

"I will start from the beginning of my journey. Please believe that everything I am about to tell you is true ... even the impossible."

"I know," said Zed.

Max began to tell his story.

UP

"One year ago today, I made a promise to myself. It was a decision—the most difficult decision I had ever made. I decided that I would discover why the maze was designed as it is; I would discover why the cheese moved; and I would discover who moved the cheese. At the time, I had no reason to believe that I would be able to discover these things. I only knew that I had to spend my life trying.

"For weeks, I spent time talking with other mice, especially the elders. I asked each of them whether they knew the answers to my questions. Not one of them did. And not one of them understood why I was asking. To them, curiosity is natural in a young mouse, but it doesn't mean that mice have the ability to satisfy their curiosity. That is what they told me: Not all questions that begin with *why* have answers—and even if they did, it was not for mice to know. It was not for mice to question. It was for mice to accept. But, you see, Zed, I could not.

"Finally, I came to the same conclusion that all other young mice come to. I concluded that a mouse in the maze could never understand *why*. But, unlike other mice, I did not do the next logical thing—which is to stop wondering why.

"Instead, realizing that there is only so much that a mouse in the maze can know and understand . . . I resolved to get *out* of the maze.

"At first, even the idea of it seemed nonsensical.

What did it even mean to get *out* of the maze? Was there such a thing? But, try as I might to reach a different decision, my passion drew me to this conclusion. And so, I began to explore how this might happen.

"I already knew that there were edges to the maze—walls beyond which there were no passages. I tried to figure out ways to break through these walls. It was impossible. I tried to dig through the floor, wondering if there was a world beneath the ground. Again I failed.

"I concluded that the only way out . . . was 'up.'

"Now, most mice never bother to look in any direction other than straight, left, right, and down—and even down is a direction that only matters when we want to find the last crumbs of cheese after a meal. Of course, as kids, we often extended our necks in the opposite direction from down and looked curiously toward the source of light. But we soon discovered that it was of no value, so we stopped bothering to do so.

"I decided that it might be worth taking another look. And, as one might expect, there was nothing to see. The walls seemed to extend indefinitely upward. But I did not give up. I looked up from every spot in the maze. I did this for days. And then it struck me. I discovered something.

"I noticed that if you stood in a passage and measured the length of the wall's shadow, and then stood in a parallel passage and measured the shadow of that wall—from the same direction—the shadows were of slightly different lengths. What this meant, of course, was that the light source was in the direction of the first wall, and that the walls were not infinitely high. There is nothing shocking about this. But, after reflecting on the problem for a number of days, I discovered that I could compute the angles at which the light was entering each passage by measuring the lengths of the shadows, the distance between the walls of the two passages, and the distance between either of the walls and another parallel wall that had no shadow. This was not easy, because there are only a few places in the maze where one can find three walls that are parallel to each other, and where the arrangement is such that one of the walls produces no shadow on either side. But then, finding this spot, making some additional reasonable assumptions, and calculating the angles, I could determine the height of the walls!

"I did the calculations and discovered the height. It would take about four mice standing on top of each other to reach the top. I recruited other mice but soon discovered that mice are not strong enough to bear the weight of more than one mouse standing on top of them. That was a problem.

"I then started to accumulate cheese—as much as I could find. I started to stack it all in a pile. But it was no use. It was not strong enough to hold my weight. Each time I tried to climb on top of the stack, I found myself in the middle of it, covered with cheese.

"I even tried to scale the walls using my claws. Again I failed.

"But then, just as I was running out of ideas, I had an encounter. It was an encounter with a mouse like no other I had ever met. A mouse who defied all logic. A mouse who was perhaps uniquely capable of solving my problem . . .

"It was a mouse named Big."

BIG

It was not his real name, but everyone called him Big. The reason was quite obvious: he was big. He was by no means the largest mouse in the maze. He was not genetically predisposed to being as large as some mice are. But he was the strongest mouse in the maze. It was not even a contest—he was the strongest mouse any other mouse could have imagined. And he was big because he wanted to be big—and because he worked at it.

It is rare to see a mouse exercising. It is practically unheard of in the maze. There is no reason for it—obtaining cheese is hardly ever a test of strength. In any case, Big did not eat very much. While a mouse will typically eat any and all cheese that he can find, Big ate just enough to support his growth. There was often cheese left on the ground after Big completed his meals. This was strange to other mice. For them, a meal was over only when there was no more cheese left to eat.

Unlike others, Big never even went in search of food. He never had to do so. If he went to eat and found that the cheese had been moved, he wasn't bothered. His daily workout involved enough running through the maze that he invariably ran into new piles of cheese every few hours. On the rare occasion that he did not find any cheese, he would simply not eat. His friends would ask him, "Why don't you go look for cheese today?"

He would reply plainly, "That's not the game I'm playing."

They would go without him.

So why work so hard to build muscle? Why spend so much time exercising? Why bother? What was the *purpose*? Big had been asked these questions his entire life.

Usually, he did not provide an answer. When he did, he would state simply, "I am the purpose."

No one bothered asking him what he meant.

Big was content. He had discovered what made him happy. And he did exactly that. He did not care if others understood. It did not matter that others would find no happiness in his pursuit. This was for him. For other mice, it would be different. And that, to Big, was entirely OK.

Big did not notice that he was in a maze. It was irrelevant to him. It imposed no restrictions on him. He had many friends and plenty of time to spend with them. More importantly, his environment provided him with ample opportunity to pursue his passion—to find peace and happiness. So he did not bother to consider the maze.

Until ...

Well, one day Big realized that something had changed in his life. And he found himself, for the first time, considering the maze—noticing its existence. But we will get to that story later. Sometime before that happened, Big met Max.

And that is where we are in Max's telling of his story.

OUT

Max continued his tale.

"Big came to me one day and said that he had heard I was attempting something crazy. He smiled as he said the word *crazy*, as if to emphasize his indifference to the term. I did not know Big—I had never even heard of him—but the sight of him was stunning. I have never seen a mouse so strong—so complete. When he told me his name was Big, I had to smile.

"Big told me that he had overheard some mice talking about 'this fella Max' who was pursuing an impossible goal. He became interested when he heard one of the mice say that I should quit being a child and go find some cheese. When another mouse added roughly that I was in my own little world, playing by my own rules, and that I was setting a bad example for the younger mice, Big decided he had to come and see me.

"Big was not interested in why I wanted to scale the wall. He did not ask me whether I thought it was possible. Instead, he asked me how high I estimated the wall to be.

"I told him it was as high as four mice.

"After a moment, he stated, 'I think I can help you.'

"I asked him how he could help. I thought about what his answer might be, but the idea of it seemed far-fetched.

"That didn't stop Big from proposing it.

"'I can throw you up there. How does that sound?'

"Unfeasible as it sounded, I knew that Big meant what he said.

"Only two words came to mind. 'Thank you,' I responded with deep appreciation.

"'Let's get moving then,' suggested Big with a smile.

"Big positioned himself so that he was standing on his hind legs with his back to the wall. He asked me to run toward him as fast as possible and then to jump up as I reached him. I did as I was told. I ran as fast as I could, and then I jumped. The moment I reached the height of my jump, I felt Big reach beneath my hind legs, and with a powerful lift, he propelled me upward. Before I knew it, my eyes were level with the top of the wall, and just as I was beginning to fall back down, I reached for the wall and grabbed it. I pulled myself up and carefully balanced myself on the thin width of the wall.

"There I was . . . A mouse who was no longer in the maze. A mouse who at that moment could see farther than any mouse had ever dreamed possible. A mouse who was about to answer the question that countless before him had posed but had eventually relinquished as impossible: Who moved my cheese?

"And I was not going to stop there."

WHO MOVED MY CHEESE?

Max continued his story.

"There are other 'beings' out there. They are like mice, but bigger. They are smarter than most mice but not as smart as some. They are called *people*. Some of these people created the maze, and it exists for their pleasure and profit—for their purposes.

"Our world—that which is our *given*—is no such thing. It is not a given outside the maze. It is designed. Its design suits the needs and interests of those who are in control. These people are the ones who give shape to our maze. They create our rules and provide our rewards and punishments. They can do this because we love cheese more than anything else. They can do this because we are mice in a maze. And for a mouse in a maze, it is all about the cheese.

"Since my first expedition outside the maze—I have had many since—I have learned a tremendous amount. I spent many months learning the language of people. I listened to them and read what they wrote. I discovered that our maze is one of many. There are other mice and other beings. While all beings are different, they are also similar in some ways.

"We need a certain amount of cheese to sustain us. But I have learned that our pursuit is not fueled by a desire to have more cheese. In fact, *having* more cheese does not make us happier—only *getting* more cheese matters to us. When we obtain a certain amount, we get used to it—and so we want more.

"Life in the maze conditions us so that no amount of cheese will ever satisfy a mouse. Happiness and peace—these are what we spend our lives pursuing as we run through the maze. But when we reach our destination, we do not find them. We only find more cheese. Again and again, the cheese fails to live up to its promise. And yet we refuse to question our beliefs about cheese, or about what will actually bring us happiness. Instead, we gear up and go looking for more cheese. And the pursuit continues.

"Earlier today, Zed, you asked the gathered crowd: *Is it possible to pursue happiness if the pursuit itself does not make you happy?*

"How many mice have the courage to answer that question? How many will be able to accept what the answer implies we should do?

You are asking mice to do things they have never learned. You are asking them to question and to *think*, but they choose to accept things as given. You are asking them to find *themselves*, but they are busy finding cheese. You are asking them to run their *lives*, but they are busy running the maze.

"You, Zed, are asking them to *be*. But they have learned only to do.

"But we mice are not alone in this. All beings are like this. Even people. They also have their mazes. They also have their cheese. But they don't use those names. They have discovered something about mice, but they do not see that their lives are similar. They, too, accept the maze as a given and see the walls as insurmountable. They, too, refuse to take action. They, too, fail to ask the most important questions.

"I have discovered that it is not irrelevant or impractical to ask, 'Who moved my cheese?' It must be known. Because it can be controlled. Indeed, it is controlled. But mice in a maze do not control it. For mice who have accepted their maze as a given—as a prison—there is no decision but to react to the designs of others. But for those who refuse to accept the maze as a given, who will challenge its design, there is another possibility: the decision to act.

"And so I have acted. I was told there is no answer to the question *why*. I was told there is no choice but to accept change. I was told to pursue only cheese. I was told that the pursuit of cheese is a given. I was told that my place is in the maze, and that the maze is a given.

"Well, I have proven otherwise.

"And that's not all . . . there is one more thing I have done.

"I was taught that if anyone ever asks aloud in frustration or confusion, "Who moved my cheese?" then I should tell that mouse it doesn't matter who moved it; it only matters that the cheese is gone.

"Well, I now have a different response to that question. The next time a mouse asks aloud, 'Who moved my cheese?' I am going to *answer* that question.

"But the answer is not what you might think, Zed—because things are different now . . . I changed them.

"My answer to the mouse will be this: *I* moved your cheese."

I MOVED YOUR CHEESE

"Once I learned the language of people, I spent much of my time studying them. I also read what they wrote about the maze. I learned how they designed it and for what purpose. I learned why they moved the cheese and how they decided where to move it. Many of the questions I had asked since childhood were answered. I discovered why there are so many useless paths in the maze, and why there are so many different ways to get to the same place.

"I learned all of this, and it explained why things work the way they do in the maze. But it did not *justify* it. In fact, there was no justice in it whatsoever. Those who had designed the maze had done so for their own benefit and for their own purposes. But they did not live in the maze. We did. I came to understand the *why*, but I was unwilling to accept it.

"So I decided to do something about it.

"Discovering how to do it took only a few weeks. Each night, the administrators who designed our maze left instructions for their assistants. In the morning, the assistants read the instructions and made the appropriate changes to the maze. They then studied the mice all afternoon and noted their observations in a logbook. In the evening, the administrators read the data provided by their assistants and decided on the instructions for the following day. The same cycle repeated every day. It was all very mundane.

"That's when I stepped in.

"I started to change what the administrators described in their instructions, and then what the assistants noted in their logbook. In this way, I was able to affect the changes that were made in the maze. I started out slowly. In the beginning, I made only small changes— moving one wall at a time, usually in a remote passage of the maze. Eventually, I became bolder. I redesigned the maze almost com- pletely. The maze is now more efficient and its design more inspiring. There is now more cheese in the maze, although it is not always easier to find.

"Why do this? What was my purpose? To help mice see the maze for what it is. To give them more time to evaluate the paths they are taking. To encourage them to think. To moti- vate them to discover what their happiness really depends on. To encourage them to discover their own purpose.

"But do you see the irony? Try as I may to help other mice, the result is still a maze that is based on my preferences and that serves my purpose—*not theirs.* The mice in the maze are no freer today than they were before! The new maze is better than the old maze, but the mice are still subject to the rules of others.

"But this does not have to be.

"If a single mouse decided, on her own, that she was no longer going to blindly pursue cheese, she would be free. I would have no control over her. My rules would be irrelevant.

"If a single mouse decided, as I decided months ago, to leave the maze, she would be free.

"If a single mouse proclaimed, as you did earlier today, that there are more interesting and important things to ponder than cheese, she would be free.

"Tell all of this to a mouse in the maze. How do you suppose he will respond? If he believes that no one can achieve greatness, then he will thank you for showing him that it is possible. However, there are also mice who *hope* that greatness is not achievable—because this alone helps justify their unquestioning ways. Tell such a mouse that greatness is possible, and he will hate you for it.

"I believe that the hunger for inspiration is greater than the hunger for cheese. But even if I am wrong, I cannot allow a maze that teaches mice that they are small and unimportant. I cannot allow a maze that teaches mice that there is nobility or wisdom in weakness and suffering. I cannot allow a maze that makes the pursuit of cheese a given. I cannot allow a maze that tells a young mouse that she cannot know or cannot achieve. I was a young mouse in exactly such a maze. And I will not allow it.

"And *that* is my pursuit.

"You are the first mouse with whom I share this because I know you will understand. And the reason I know this is simple . . .

"I moved the cheese for all sorts of mice in the maze—and I influenced them. By moving their cheese, I changed how they thought, what they felt, which direction they traveled, and what they believed.

"I moved *your* cheese, too, Zed—many times. And you simply did not care."

WALLS

Max had finished his tale. The look on his face suggested that he was content. He wanted nothing from Zed. He was not seeking approval. He was not looking for a specific reaction.

"Thank you for sharing your story with me," said Zed. "Yours is truly a remarkable journey. You are a mouse like no other."

It was now dark.

"Let's talk more tomorrow," Zed suggested. "It is getting late. Will you meet me here in the morning?"

"Yes," said Max.

Max expected Zed to get up and walk past him down the passage. Instead, Zed turned toward the corner and began to walk straight toward the wall. Max looked at him, confused. This was a dead end. Was Zed planning on staying here, in the corner, for the night? Had he become disoriented?

Zed kept walking.

It was perhaps a moment before Zed walked headfirst into the wall that Max opened his mouth to shout a warning: "Stop!"

And then he saw it happen.

Before his very eyes, Max saw Zed walk *through* the wall. He walked through it as if the wall were not even there ... as if the wall were made of nothing but air ... as if the wall simply did not matter. And he was gone. Max stood there, staring blankly at the wall.

A moment later, he heard Zed's voice from the other side of the wall.

"You were right, Max," he said. "It *is* possible to be free. And tomorrow, I will tell you *my* story."

Max sat down, utterly stunned. He knew Zed was smiling. He had to smile back.

"And *I* have been the one talking this whole time," Max thought to himself in amusement.

THE MAZE IN THE MOUSE

Max arrived at their meeting place early the next morning. He had not slept all night. But he felt more awake—more alive—than ever. He noticed that he was looking down the long passage in anticipation of Zed. He had to laugh.

Any other mouse would have to walk down that passage to come here, he thought. But Zed did not. He did not have to do anything. He could appear from anywhere.

And then he saw Zed walking toward him, as any other mouse would, down the long passage. And he laughed again.

Once they had greeted each other and were seated, Zed spoke.

"Yesterday, Max, before you started your story, you told me that everything you were going to tell me was true. 'Even the impossible.'"

"That's right," agreed Max.

"Well," said Zed, "let *me* start by saying that nothing I will tell you is impossible."

Max nodded.

Zed went on. "What would you say if I told you that there was no difference—none—between what you accomplished when you exited the maze and what I did last night?"

"I would say that it may be true, but I don't see how it is possible," replied Max.

"Max, how did you exit the maze?" asked Zed.

"I reached for the top of the wall. I pulled myself

up. And then I climbed out. I had help. Big was there to help me up," answered Max.

"All of that is true. But go back further in your story. Why are you the only mouse that has ever exited the maze? Why was Big there to help *you*? How did you get to a point in your life where you were reaching for the top of a wall?"

Max thought for a moment. Then he answered. "I was the only one trying to get out."

"So what, *essentially*, is the reason for your accomplishment?"

"My decision. My resolve. My *thought*. The thought that I would escape."

"And everything else followed from that," added Zed.

"Yes."

"You had a thought. And that thought directed actions that gave physical shape to your thought—to your vision. It is the same with me. I did what I thought I could do. I did what I decided was the way it had to be. I do not think about the maze, or its walls, the way most others do. You and I have that in common."

"But there is a difference," said Max. "What I did was . . . possible. What you did . . . physically, or however . . . is not . . . It defies everything we know. It's not supposed to be."

"Then there is no difference at all," said Zed. "There's not a mouse in the maze who thought it was possible for you to accomplish what you did. It transcended *their* thinking, but not yours."

"I agree. But, still, there is a difference. I can explain to you how I escaped the maze. I have done so. Can you explain to me—describe to me—how you walked through that wall?"

"Yes. I can explain it," answered Zed. "Everything that happens—everything that we do—stems from our thoughts. Consider physical pursuits: if we want to reach for a piece of cheese, our thinking directs our body to move toward the cheese. Although our thoughts and body are not physically connected, the body reacts because the mind *insists* it is possible to move the body in specific and meaningful ways. Watch a newborn mouse and you will see that such conviction is not something we are born with, but something we must cultivate through sustained practice and reflection. It's the same with our other pursuits—those that are not physical. If we focus on solving a problem, there is no physical connection between the intention to accomplish this goal, the mental effort that follows, and the ultimate solution. What allows us to go from problem to analysis to solution is the insistence of the mind. This is what must be understood—what must be realized. *This* is the explanation, for all of it: there is no physical continuity anywhere, and *everything* stems from the insistence of the mind."

Max looked at him attentively, considering the words.

Zed continued. "It doesn't matter whether *you* think that you can walk through walls. After all, you found your own way to escape the maze. But you should realize that the same process was in play when you went farther than any other mouse you had ever encountered. You refused to accept the assumptions, the rules, and the constraints that others had accepted. You were able to have the thought—and to develop the conviction—that you could know more and do more. And so you went about doing it. I did the same. I challenged assumptions. I broke rules. I ignored constraints. I refused to believe that *anything* was a given. The result was inevitable. The maze ceased to exist."

"Then . . . it does not really exist?" asked Max. "For anyone?"

"It does. For most mice, it does. They define themselves—their very existence—in reference to the maze. You have said it many times yourself—you have described them as mice in the maze. That statement isn't false, but it is dangerously misleading."

"How so?" asked Max.

Zed smiled.

"You see, Max, the problem is not that the mouse is in the maze, but that the maze is in the mouse."

A MOUSE LIKE NO OTHER

Max and Zed had sat together now, in silence, for almost an hour. Neither had more to say. Neither was in any rush to leave.

Max was thinking—his mind was working to understand, to capture, all that Zed had just explained to him. He knew that it would be a long time before he could *realize*—to make real for himself—what he was beginning to comprehend. But the conversation had left him energized. He was happy.

Zed was also thinking. He was thinking about the incredible mouse sitting before him, who had managed to climb out of the maze and take control of his world. He had learned something from Max—something he had never cared to know before. But, know-ing it now, he was amused . . . It had been Max, working away in the logbook outside the maze, who had placed that fresh piece of cheese he found next to his bed each morning.

After some time, the two mice parted. They would meet again as friends.

Each would continue to follow his own path. But each would be helped along in his jour-ney—strengthened by the knowledge of the other . . . knowing that somewhere in the maze—or beyond—there was a mouse like no other.

SOME MICE ARE BIG

It was a day like any other for Big. He woke up, stretched, and then began his morning run. He ran through the maze—fast—following his usual path. He normally ran for an hour, and then shifted his attention to strength training.

Big had used a single criterion when he first decided to chart out the path he would follow during his morning runs. Big wanted to sprint at maximum speed through the maze and did not want the hassle of having to dodge crowds of other mice. His path consisted of the least crowded passages in the maze.

But on this day, Big noticed that something had changed. The passages he was running through—the ones he had always run through—were crowded. After he finished his run, he reflected on this. He realized that the population of mice in the maze had been increasing, slowly, for quite some time. He had noticed this earlier, in some parts of the maze, but never thought much about the trend until today. Today, it had affected his run.

Something had to be done about it. Big spent the afternoon walking through the maze, exploring it fully. He paid special attention to the more remote passages. After he felt that he had seen enough, he considered his options.

The path he had followed in the past was still one of the best. Some improvements could be made, of course, and it seemed like a good idea to make them. Big worked on the problem for an hour, until he was satisfied that he had mapped out the best path for his run. He looked at the map. It was good. But it wasn't great.

The path he charted out could work—for a while. But soon even the more remote passages would become crowded—not tremendously crowded, but enough to slow him down. That was unacceptable.

He reflected on the situation. He found himself considering, for the first time in his life, the maze. He had never before given it any thought. It had been irrelevant to him. But now its design, its very existence, was standing in the way of his pursuit. He could not accept that.

The maze was big. But it was not big enough.

The maze was a way of life. But it was not his way of life.

The maze was all he had ever known. But it was not all he could imagine.

The decision was made.

It was late in the evening. Big walked toward one of the edges of the maze. When he reached the wall, he touched it gently. He took a step back. Then he thrust forward with all his might . . . and punched straight through the wall.

Big stepped through the hole he had created and walked out of the maze. He would never return to it. The maze was, once again, irrelevant.

Some pursuits are simply too important.

Some lives are not so easily contained.

Some mice are big.

THE BEGINNING

DISCUSSION QUESTIONS

I hope you enjoyed the story and that it inspires you to reconsider some of the things that are often taken for granted in your environment. Some of you may look forward to sharing thoughts and reactions with friends or members of your book club. Others may see the book as a tool for structuring discussion and analysis with members of an organization. This section of the book is designed to help foster continued reflection and discussion.

I believe that each reader will naturally extract from a book what is most important to him- or herself. The questions below are not designed to guide or structure your discussion, but rather to get the ball rolling. Feel free to start with any question, to jump around without regard to the order of the questions, or to ignore the lists altogether.

The first list of questions is for those who wish to engage in personal reflection. As Max, Zed, and Big would tell us, personal reflection is the most important aspect of growth and learning. And yet it can also be helpful to hear how others interpreted the story and what insights they drew from it. They may have focused on something you missed; you may have deciphered a certain lesson that they, too, would benefit from considering. The other lists of questions were motivated by these considerations.

Whether you are sitting with a group of friends, in a conference room with colleagues, or in a classroom with fellow students, a discussion regarding the adventures of Max, Big, and Zed may allow you to define and refine your own thoughts. Challenging each other's interpretation of an episode may also lead to novel conclusions that no one person reached alone. Hearing what lessons each person drew can also encourage greater appreciation for the variety of perspectives, problems, and solutions different people have encountered in their lives.

REFLECTION QUESTIONS
FOR INDIVIDUALS

1. Describe the key traits of Max, Big, and Zed. Which characteristics are most impressive? Which would be most useful to you if you cultivated them?

2. Who would you most like as a boss: Max, Big, or Zed? Who would you most like as a colleague, or as someone who reports to you? As a friend? Why?

3. Can you think of a time you walked through a wall when no one else thought it was possible? Can you think of a time you escaped from a maze when no one else thought to even pursue that objective? If so, how did you do it? If not, what has kept you from doing so?

4. What are some of the mazes in which you find yourself today? Are they of your choosing? Would you like to escape? How can you do that in a positive, productive way?

5. In the chapter titled "Big," what does Big mean when he says, "That's not the game I'm playing"? What game is Big playing?

6. What game are you playing? Is it the right game for you?

7. If you told Max about your life, what advice would he give you?

8. If you told Zed about your greatest concerns or fears, what would he say?

9. Are there mazes that you have created for other people? Are there people in your life who are pursuing paths and chasing goals that are of your design, not theirs? Is that fair or reasonable? If so, why? If not, what should you or they do differently?

10. Who in your life would most benefit from hearing about Max, Big, and Zed? Why?

DISCUSSION QUESTIONS FOR GROUPS AND BOOK CLUBS

1. What are some of the mazes in which you, or people you care about, seem to be running? How would you describe these mazes? Who designed them? What keeps people running? Would they benefit from an escape?

2. In the chapter titled "The Maze in the Mouse," what does Zed mean when he says: "You see, Max, the problem is not that the mouse is in the maze, but that the maze is in the mouse"? Do you think this is true? If so, how does that happen? Can you think of mazes that people believe are external but that are really inside the person? How can we escape them?

3. Max, Big, and Zed escape the maze—and each of them does it in a unique way. What traits does each mouse represent? What can we learn from the approach that each of these mice pursued?

4. Do you think Max could have escaped the maze without Big's help?

5. Have you, or anyone you know, ever walked through a wall? How? What does it take? Why can't everyone do it?

6. What do you think of Zed's explanation for his abilities? Does it make sense to you? Do you believe what Zed believes?

7. Why doesn't Zed walk through walls all the time?

8. Do you think other mice will escape the maze? Or is this not possible for everyone? Why?

9. Why does Max return to the maze after all that he has learned?

10. What do you most agree and disagree with in the book's message?

DISCUSSION QUESTIONS
FOR YOUR ORGANIZATION
(OR TEAM)

1. If Max were to study your organization, what would he say? What advice would he give?

2. If Zed were asked to evaluate the assumptions in your organization—those things that are taken for granted—what would be his evaluation? What advice would he give?

3. Why were so many of the other mice in the maze uncomfortable with the issues that Max and Zed raised? Clearly, many of these mice had overcome the fear of change. What was the fear that remained?

4. How would you describe the strengths of Max, Big, and Zed? Which of these

strengths do you think are prevalent in your organization? Which of them are under-represented? How can these strengths be cultivated?

5. What are the mazes that exist within your organization, or in your organization's environment? Who designed them? Why do they persist? What are the taken-for-granted goals—your equivalent of the pursuit of cheese—that may be worth reconsidering?

6. What, precisely, stands in the way of changing things in your organization? Are there things that can and should be changed immediately? Are there things that cannot be changed in the short run but that can and should be changed over time? Are there steps that need to be taken today to ensure positive change in the future?

7. Would people with traits like those of Max, Big, or Zed be successful in your organization? Why—or why not?

8. Would Max, Big, and Zed make good leaders? If so, why does no one seem to be following them?

9. What leadership qualities, if any, do you see in Max, Big, and Zed? Which are the hardest to acquire?

10. What would be your organization's equivalent of asking "ridiculous" questions like, "Why is there a maze?" Can ridiculous questions can be safely asked and seriously considered in your organization? Would your organization benefit from asking such questions more often?

A NOTE TO EDUCATORS

Like many of you, I love to teach, and I am constantly looking for better ways to make a positive difference in the lives of students. It would be easy if the goal were simply to provide facts and findings, or to present strategies and frameworks. For many of us, it is at least as important—and perhaps more important—to motivate deeper analyses, inspire greater reflection, and equip students with the habits of mind that will allow them to continue learning and developing once they leave the classroom. My hope is that this book will help in our efforts to do some of these more difficult things. That is the goal. Now for two practical considerations:

First, which students would benefit from

reading this book? In my discussions with students and educators, I have heard two kinds of answers. One group informs me that courses in the fields of leadership, organizational behavior, power and politics, entrepreneurship, and strategy are most likely to benefit from a discussion inspired by this book. Another group informs me that some of the biggest mistakes students make in their lives pertain to the majors they choose and the jobs they pursue; that many of these choices reflect external pressures and expectations rather than a careful evaluation by the student of his or her own goals and passions. Sadly, many students will spend a few years—and some a lifetime—pursuing dreams that are not their own. This book may be helpful in encouraging students to tackle these issues earlier in their journey.

Second, I am aware of the cost of introducing

new material into a course or a program. We need to figure out where this material belongs and how to develop a lesson plan. In this regard, my advice is to trust the students. While there are discussion questions in the book, many of which could be used to initiate and guide classroom conversation, this is the kind of book for which *less teaching will lead to more learning*. Once the book is assigned, students will do most of the heavy lifting. In my experience, those are the sessions that students remember.

A NOTE TO MANAGERS AND EXECUTIVES

Over the last decade, I have taught approximately ten thousand business owners, executives, and managers. Most of this teaching has taken place at Harvard Business School, where I have taught extensively in MBA as well as executive education courses. A large portion of the teaching has also taken place in-house during consulting and training visits to organizations around the world in almost every industry. While most of my teaching and consulting has focused on negotiation and strategic decision making, I have also had the opportunity to engage in deep discussion on a wide range of problems that managers and executives deal with, often daily:

- How can we inspire our employees?

- How should we structure incentives?

- How do we create a culture of innovation?

- How can we recruit the best talent?

- How can we develop the best leaders?

- How can we differentiate ourselves in our industry and in the eyes of customers?

- How can we assert greater control in an environment where we are often at the mercy of economic and competitive forces that are beyond our control?

- What kind of organizational structure is best suited to the goals we are pursuing?

- Are we focusing on the wrong goals?

I hope that this book will help you target some of these questions and concerns. The vast majority of managers and executives that I have worked with are smart and hard-working, and they have good intentions—and yet they continue to struggle with these kinds of problems. The reason is that intellect, effort, and intent are necessary—but not sufficient—to solve some of the more vexing problems we face. We also need to step back and challenge our assumptions, to see the old in new ways, to try not only harder but also differently, and above all, to create an environment where people are constantly asking *why* and *why not*. I hope this book helps you and your colleagues to create such an environment in your organization.

QUESTIONS TO THE AUTHOR

1. *What will happen to Max, Big, and Zed?*

   We have not heard the last of these three mice. There are a few things I can say about what happens next: The adventures of Max, Big, and Zed continue outside the maze, but there are also more mazes to visit. Their lives intersect again and in more interesting ways. New characters enter the story. The plot thickens.

2. *What was the inspiration for these three characters?*

   The story began with Max, who was born almost instantly after I read *Who Moved My Cheese?* (*WMMC*) for the first time. He came to embody my intellectual and affective response to *WMMC*. Of course, his story could not be written until he had grown up quite a bit—which is to say, until the intellectual and affective response could mature. Once Max was old enough to start causing some trouble, he met Zed and Big. Zed and Big had always been there, in the maze, so to speak, but their stories were more difficult to articulate. We needed Max to bring everything together and to start the necessary dialogues. Each of them became, very quickly, indispensable to me, because I discovered that this was one story, not three stories. Max's story was incomplete in the way that intellectual and affective responses to a situation are often incomplete.

3. *Who is your favorite character?*
    When thinking about this in general terms,

it is a little bit like choosing between your children; you love them all equally. On the other hand, while reading the story itself, I find that the character I'm most impressed with varies, depending on what I'm going through or thinking about in my life at that time.

4. *Who is the hardest character to write about?*
Zed. (But sometimes it is Big.)

ACKNOWLEDGMENTS

I am grateful to many people—many of whom have influenced the making of this book.

At Harvard University, I am surrounded by fantastic colleagues who inspire excellence. I am fortunate to work in an environment and culture that encourages not only the development of new ideas but also the transformation of ideas into action.

I was introduced to my publisher, Berrett-Koehler, by two former students, Ethan Willis and Randy Garn. Thank you, Ethan and Randy, for setting in motion the process that led to the publication of this book. At Berrett-Koehler, I have had the pleasure of working with an amazing team of professionals. I am especially thankful to Steve Piersanti for his early (and ever-growing) enthusiasm for what I had written, and his great insights on everything related to the business of books. Thanks also to Jeevan Sivasubramaniam, Kristen Frantz, Dianne Platner, Maria Jesus Aguilo, and the many other folks at B-K who put so much of their time, energy, and expertise into this project.

I would also like to thank the many amazing teachers I have had in my life. I learned much more than I could have bargained for each time I entered Mr. Leider's theater class in high school, Sifu Brown's school of martial arts as a newly minted college grad, and Professor Murnighan's office as a young scholar at the Kellogg School of Management. To these, and the many other great teachers I've encountered, I am eternally grateful.

Finally, and most of all, I am indebted to

my family. My parents, Chander and Sudesh Malhotra, demonstrated to me the value of charting one's own path in life and, more importantly, encouraged my every idea, ambition, and endeavor. My brother, Manu Malhotra, has walked through enough walls in his life that I wonder whether he even notices they exist. My wife, Shikha, not only gives me the strength and support to search for what lies beyond the maze, but also helps knock down the walls that I'm having a hard time scaling. My kids deserve much credit for my work: looking at my children makes me want to solve big problems.

ABOUT THE AUTHOR

DEEPAK MALHOTRA is a professor in the Negotiations, Organizations, and Markets Unit at Harvard Business School. He teaches negotiation strategy to MBA students as well as in a variety of executive programs, including the Owner/President Management Program, Changing the Game, and Families in Business. Deepak is the author (with Max Bazerman) of *Negotiation Genius: How to Overcome Obstacles and Achieve Brilliant Results at the Bargaining Table and Beyond.* It was awarded the 2008 Outstanding Book Award by the International Institute for Conflict Prevention and Resolution.

Deepak's research focuses on negotiation strategy, strategic decision making, trust development, competitive escalation, and international and ethnic dispute resolution. It has been published in top journals in the fields of management, psychology, conflict resolution, and foreign policy. His work has also received considerable media attention, including multiple appearances by Deepak on CNBC. Deepak has won awards for both his teaching and his research.

Deepak's professional activities include training, consulting, and advisory work for firms across the globe in dozens of industries. He is also a frequently invited speaker to executive groups such as the Young Presidents' Organization (YPO) and the Entrepreneurs' Organization (EO).

You can follow Deepak on Twitter at www.Twitter.com/Prof_Malhotra.

You can visit Deepak's official website at www.DeepakMalhotra.com.

Visit the website for *I Moved Your Cheese* at www.RazeTheMaze.com.

Find Deepak's book on negotiation at www.NegotiationGenius.com.

Berrett–Koehler
Publishers

Berrett-Koehler is an independent publisher dedicated to an ambitious mission: *Creating a World That Works for All*.

We believe that to truly create a better world, action is needed at all levels—individual, organizational, and societal. At the individual level, our publications help people align their lives with their values and with their aspirations for a better world. At the organizational level, our publications promote progressive leadership and management practices, socially responsible approaches to business, and humane and effective organizations. At the societal level, our publications advance social and economic justice, shared prosperity, sustainability, and new solutions to national and global issues.

A major theme of our publications is "Opening Up New Space." Berrett-Koehler titles challenge conventional thinking, introduce new ideas, and foster positive change. Their common quest is changing the underlying beliefs, mindsets, institutions, and structures that keep generating the same cycles of problems, no matter who our leaders are or what improvement programs we adopt.

We strive to practice what we preach—to operate our publishing company in line with the ideas in our books. At the core of our approach is stewardship, which we define as a deep sense of responsibility to administer the company for the benefit of all of our "stakeholder" groups: authors, customers, employees, investors, service providers, and the communities and environment around us.

We are grateful to the thousands of readers, authors, and other friends of the company who consider themselves to be part of the "BK Community." We hope that you, too, will join us in our mission.

A BK Business Book

This book is part of our BK Business series. BK Business titles pioneer new and progressive leadership and management practices in all types of public, private, and nonprofit organizations. They promote socially responsible approaches to business, innovative organizational change methods, and more humane and effective organizations.

Berrett–Koehler
Publishers

A community dedicated to creating
a world that works for all

Visit Our Website: www.bkconnection.com

Read book excerpts, see author videos and Internet movies, read
our authors' blogs, join discussion groups, download book apps, find
out about the BK Affiliate Network, browse subject-area libraries of
books, get special discounts, and more!

Subscribe to Our Free E-Newsletter, the *BK Communiqué*

Be the first to hear about new publications, special discount offers,
exclusive articles, news about bestsellers, and more! Get on the list
for our free e-newsletter by going to **www.bkconnection.com**.

Get Quantity Discounts

Berrett-Koehler books are available at quantity discounts for orders
of ten or more copies. Please call us toll-free at (800) 929-2929 or
email us at bkp.orders@aidcvt.com.

Join the BK Community

BKcommunity.com is a virtual meeting place where people from
around the world can engage with kindred spirits to create a world
that works for all. BKcommunity.com members may create their own
profiles, blog, start and participate in forums and discussion groups,
post photos and videos, answer surveys, announce and register for
upcoming events, and chat with others online in real time. Please join
the conversation!

MIX
From responsible
sources
FSC® C113845